#PILOT LIFE
A SNARKY ADULT
COLORING BOOK

PILOTS
LOOKING DOWN
ON PEOPLE
SINCE 1903

Published By Pilot Passion Publishing

This Book Belongs To

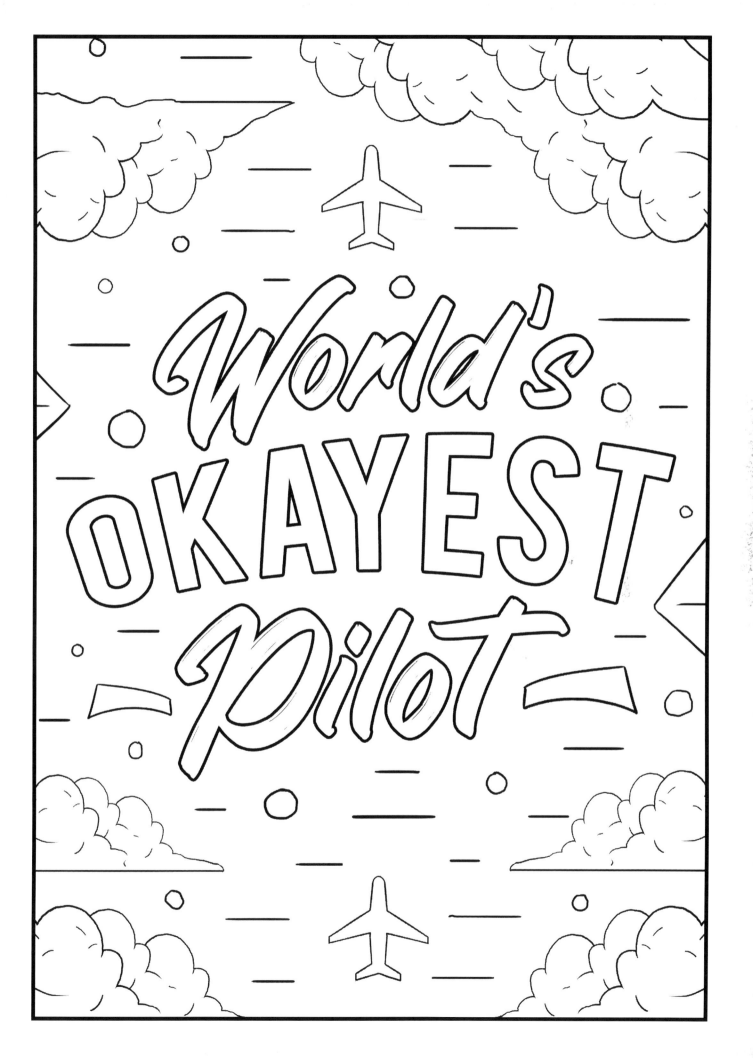

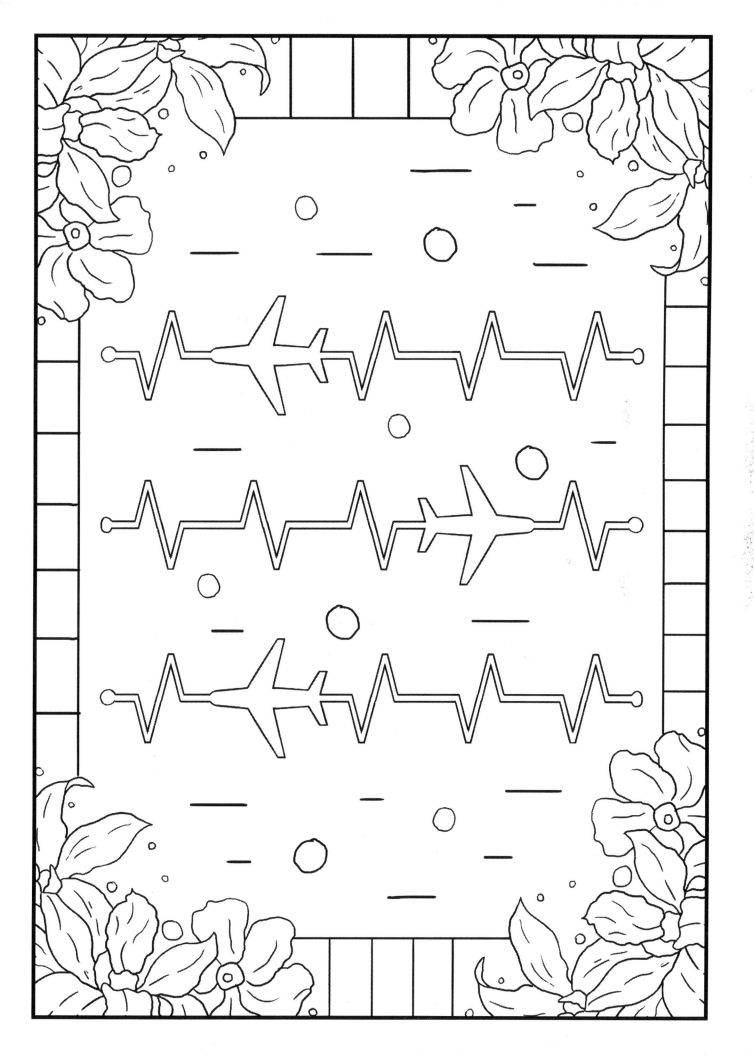

Wake Up

FLAPS 5°

FLAPS 30°

SLEEP

REPEAT

I LOVE THE SMELL OF Avgas IN THE MORNING

Made in the USA
Columbia, SC
19 May 2020